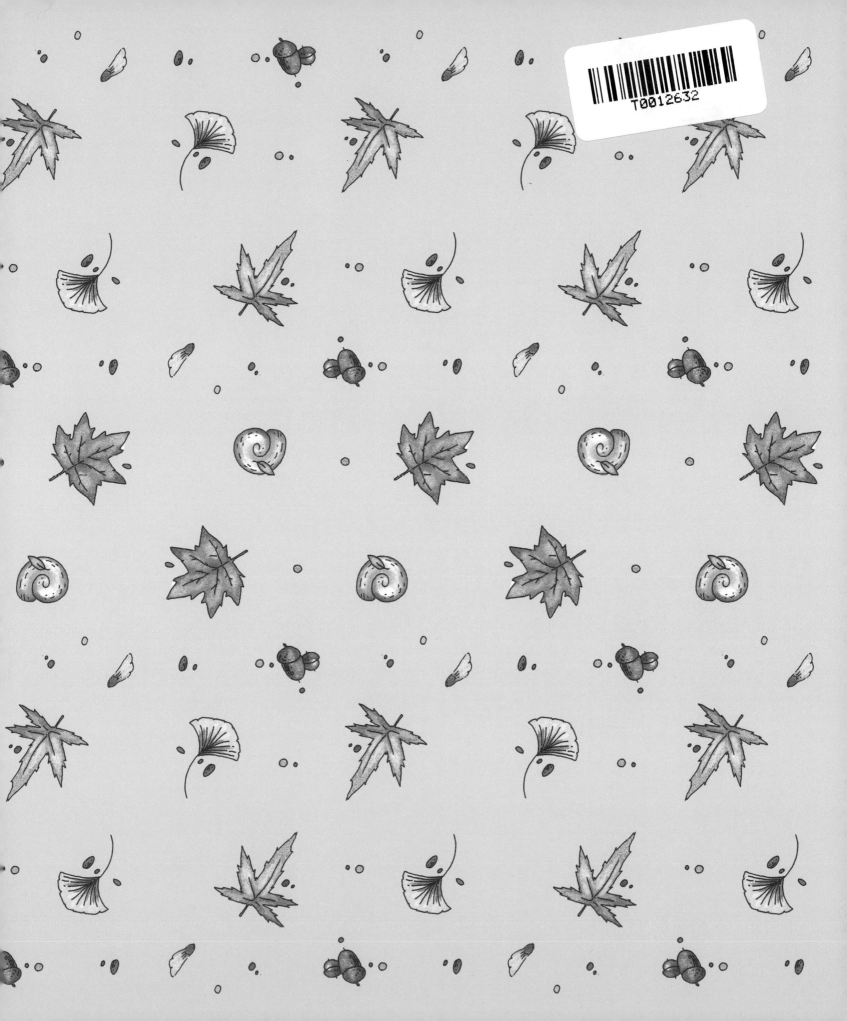

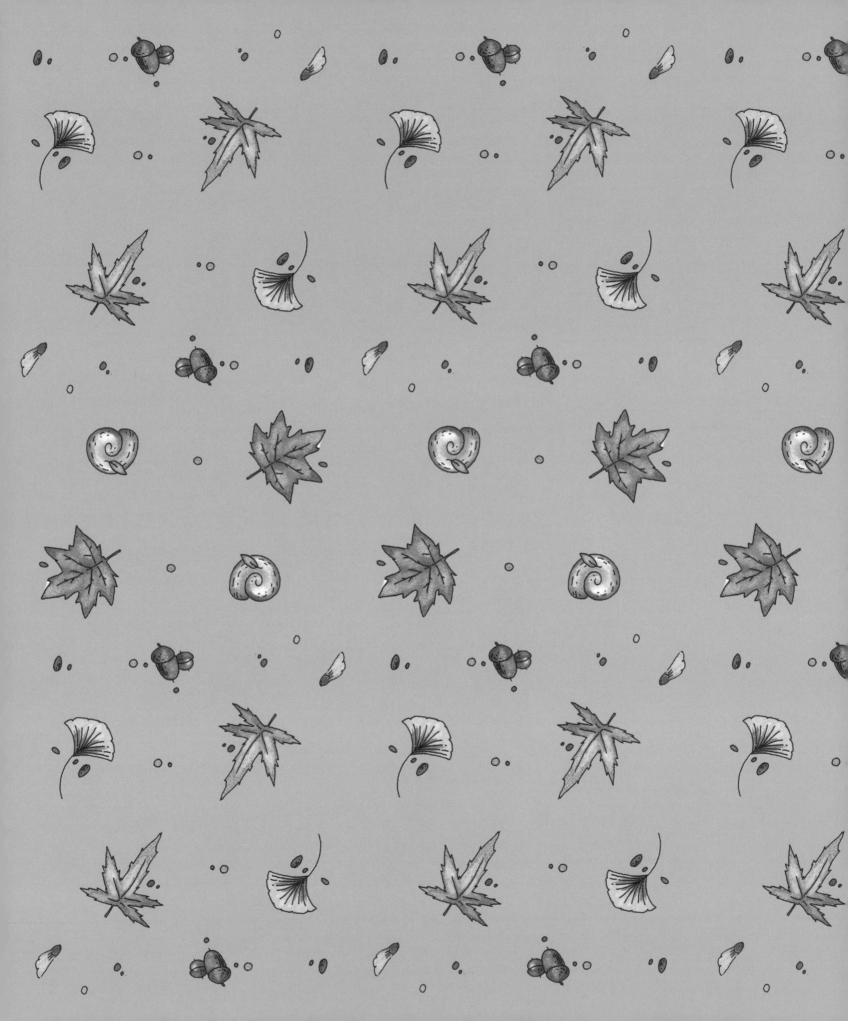

The Secret Life of the Forest

Explore the connections between trees, animals, and fungi

Table of Contents

Hi there! I'm a little linden seed. I'm going to guide you on your way through the forest realm!

Where do seeds come from?

Small as they are, they are extremely important. Who, you ask? Why, bees, of course! Without these busy little creatures, no seeds – the embryos of new trees or plants – would ever sprout. Luckily, they are not alone in this vital work …

A tree growing from a seed

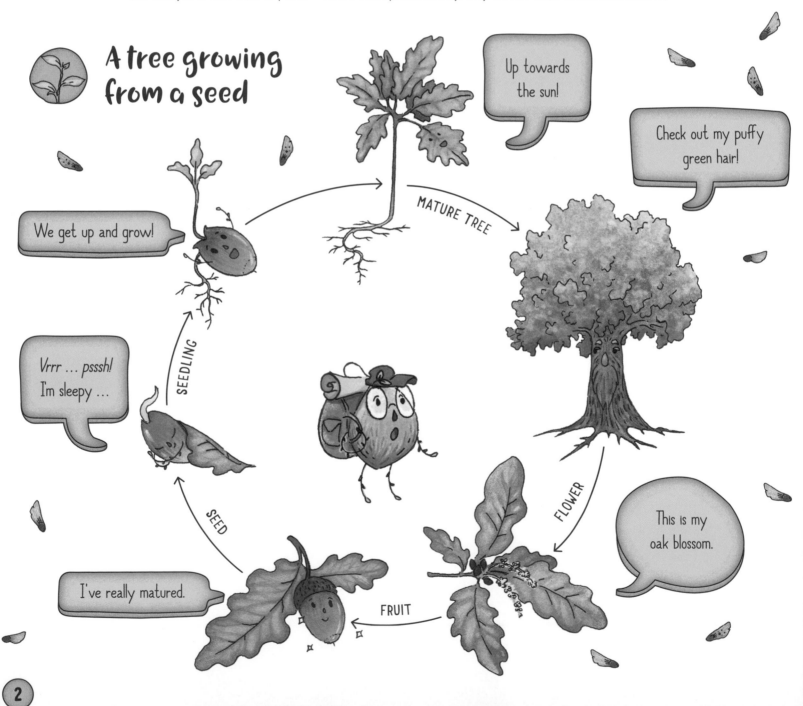

Up towards the sun!

Check out my puffy green hair!

We get up and grow!

MATURE TREE

SEEDLING

Vrrr … psssh! I'm sleepy …

FLOWER

This is my oak blossom.

SEED

I've really matured.

FRUIT

Where are you flying off to, Bee?

To pollinate bellflowers! I transfer the pollen from their stamens to the pistils ... Only 889 flowers to go!

Wow, that's a lot of pollen! I can lend you my backpack if you want.

 # Do bees need a backpack for their pollen?

Of course not. Bees don't need a backpack or a rucksack – they have grooves in their back legs where they store the pollen they collect. However, these grooves are tiny, so the bee has to make several flights to gather as much pollen as possible and **pollinate** as many plants as possible. This is very important work! Otherwise, unpollinated flowers wouldn't produce any structures like fruit, nuts, or cones to protect the small **seeds**. The bees keep some of the pollen for ... well, let's say for their own private purposes. They use it to make nutritious "royal jelly" for the offspring and the queen.

PISTIL

STAMENS

Guess who pollinates us!

Some plants can pollinate themselves with their own pollen – we call them **self-pollinating**. Others, including many conifers as well as walnuts and hazelnuts, are pollinated by the **wind**. Still others are helped by **water**. However, in order to pollinate, many plants need helpers from

Wheeee, we're flying!

the animal kingdom: **pollinators**. Did you know that nearly all the lush green beauty of the tropical rainforests is pollinated by a **variety of animals** living up in the treetops and down in the undergrowth?

1. Honeybee: We bees keep ourselves quite busy! In a single flight we can visit around a hundred flowers. Each of us makes several flights a day, so by the time the sun sets we might have pollinated a thousand flowers.

2. Bumblebee: I don't mind low temperatures, so I can start pollinating early in the spring. Mmm, this crab apple tree, for example, smells just divine!

3. Fruit fly: Can you smell that too? Something is fermenting here ... I definitely don't want to miss out on that! I love the scent of rotting fruit, especially figs, apples, and pineapples.

4. Chafer beetle: We bugs like big open flowers with lots of pollen, like this magnolia. We help to transfer its pollen and as a reward we get to stuff ourselves!

5. Ruffed lemur: As a primate that is the world's largest pollinator, I may seem slightly out of place among all these tiny little fellas, but believe it or not, I can pollinate every bit as well as them. After all, my whole life revolves around transferring pollen from the traveler's tree and drinking its nectar ...

6. Banana bat: I specialize in banana trees and cactuses. Each spring I lick the sweet nectar out of their long

BOREAL FOREST

RIPARIAN FOREST

flowers, transferring pollen in the process. Then in the summer I have a regular banana feast!

7. Honey possum: I have a long snout and a very long tongue and I like collecting the nectar from the flowers of the Australian banksia plant. The pollen that sticks to my fur is then easily transferred from the stamens to the pistil.

8. Blue-tailed day gecko: Lots of beautiful and very rare shrubs grow on the island of Mauritius. And I have

the honor and responsibility of being their one and only pollinator!

9. Monarch butterfly: With my long proboscis I pollinate the occasional orchid too. But shhhh!, not a word to my nocturnal relatives the hawkmoths, who come out for nectar when the sun goes down ...

10. Hummingbird: I flap my tiny wings so quickly I can hover in one place. Naturally, that's the perfect opportunity to grab a quick snack. My beak is as well equipped for pollinating orchids as a butterfly's proboscis. It's just a question of who gets to the flower first!

11. Blowfly: I'm a bit of a carnivore ... What I like best is the deep-red rafflesia flowers with the delightful stench of rotting meat.

TROPICAL RAINFOREST

TROPICAL DRY RAINFOREST

5

Trees – the lungs of the planet

What do trees actually need in order to grow from tiny seeds into majestic giants? The answer lies in a magic trick with a mysterious name: **photosynthesis**.

LIGHT AND CARBON DIOXIDE (CO_2)

SUGAR

OXYGEN (O_2)

WATER (H_2O)

What do trees eat?

Trees don't need all that much to eat. They make do with a bit of **light and water**. Naturally, like all living beings, they also breathe. However, unlike people, most of the time they breathe in **carbon dioxide** rather than oxygen. They use this gas, along with water, to make **sugar** (yum!), an important source of energy for their growth. And in return they breathe out **oxygen** into the air, which is then breathed in by people and animals. A one-hundred-year-old beech tree can breathe out over 250 gallons of oxygen, which is enough for three people. This mysterious process has an even more mysterious-sounding name: **photosynthesis**!

... And how do they breathe?

Trees breathe ever so quietly and only through their **green parts** – i.e., their **leaves**. None of this mysterious photosynthesis goes on in the trunk or in the roots of the tree.

Breathing at night and in winter

Photosynthesis needs light to work. So, can it happen at night? In the dark? When it's pitch black and the only light comes from the moon and the stars? And what about in winter, when the leaves have fallen from the trees – how do trees breathe then? Don't worry, the trees have got it all figured out. In winter, they go to sleep, which means they use much less oxygen than in the spring or summer. At night, trees breathe the way people do: they breathe in a little oxygen and breathe out a little carbon dioxide. Overall, though, they still breathe out more oxygen than they use up – which is why people are right to call them the **"lungs of the planet."**

How do trees make friends with each other?

Just imagine: those small, helpless seeds – without which no dense forest would ever see the light of day – all have whole tree families of their own. So it's not just adult trees we find in the forest, but also their children and their ancient ancestors.

Trees help their children

A tree community takes good care of its babies. As soon as a new seed falls to the ground, the parent tree connects to it through a network of fine roots. That's so it can **send nourishment** to it in the form of **water** and **sugar**. It knows very well that a lone seed with just one little root and a sprouting shoot is unable to get nutrients for itself – to do that, it'll need leaves, which can capture sunlight. Seeds that are carried to another forest by the wind will get help from older trees in the vicinity.

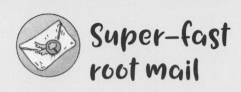

Super-fast root mail

It's not just life-giving fluids that trees send to each other through their roots. Thanks to their vast and extremely tangled network of roots, they also **communicate with each other** and can warn each other of imminent danger. For example, when a huge group of greedy bark beetles is about to descend on them or one very hungry deer has set its sights (and its teeth) on them. This vast root network links the whole forest together!

A mysterious scent

While trees talk to each other by means of a network of roots, they communicate with friends and foes from the animal kingdom using a different language: a special scent. As soon as they start to feel threatened, they release this special scent into the air and the wind carries it right under the noses of all the animals nearby. Beetles and other insects can't stand the smell of it because it's horribly bitter. Birds, on the other hand, can't get enough of it, so they immediately follow it and the scent leads them to a place teeming with delicious food.

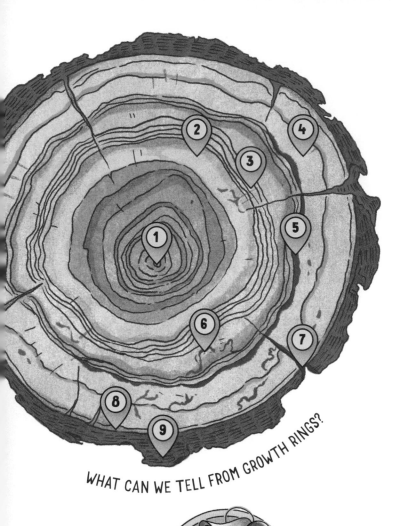

WHAT CAN WE TELL FROM GROWTH RINGS?

How old is that tree?

We can recognize old trees by their broad trunks covered with wrinkles of a rough material called **bark** – the thicker and bulkier the trunk, the older the tree is likely to be.

In a cross section of a tree we can see the lines of its **rings**. They resemble big human fingerprints. We can learn a lot from them! People even developed a special scientific discipline that deals with their mysterious reading – it's called *dendro-chronology*.

1. YEAR 1
2. A WARMER YEAR
3. A COOLER YEAR
4. A RAINY YEAR
5. A SCAR FROM A FOREST FIRE
6. IN INSECT ATTACK
7. AN EARTHQUAKE
8. INNER BARK
9. OUTER BARK

Let's experiment in the forest!

Try to calculate the age of a tree by counting its growth rings – each ring represents one year. From the color and shape of the individual rings, tree experts can even tell which year the tree suffered from a harsh winter or from insects or when, on the contrary, it had a good year.

MULTI-SPECIES FOREST

MONOCULTURE FOREST

One tree to rule them all ...

In **multi-species forests**, the different species of trees support each other, because they complement one another – sometimes a little and sometimes a lot. However, in other forests there are only trees of the same species and the same age growing. These are called **monoculture forests** (*mono* as in one species of tree). The most common type is a spruce forest, because this tree is a real sprinter – it grows very quickly – and it also has beautiful straight wood, which is why in the past people thought it was a great idea to grow it on a big scale. But later they found out that there was a problem – or rather several problems – with growing trees this way:

1) Many trees of the same species, growing too close together, compete with each other for light. In a small space, they will only grow thin trunks ...

2) ... and they are more easily attacked by pests or eaten by deer.

3) The same flowers always grow and the same animals always live under the same trees. That's why many organisms won't find conditions suitable for life in monoculture forests.

4) The root network of a single species of tree is not as strong as a network made up of different types of trees ...

5) ... and that's why single-species forests are worse at retaining water. The soil beneath them is more easily depleted, which disturbs the already fragile root system even more.

6) These trees are often planted in an environment that is unnatural for them and a lot of them will perish very soon.

Let's experiment in the forest!

Find tree stumps in the forest and try to work out which ones are living and which ones aren't. How can you tell? If the bark is peeling off and there is rotten wood inside the stump, it's already dead. But if the bark is firm and the inside is solid, the stump is still alive! How is that possible? The trees growing around it are still helping their chopped-down pal and sending it all the nutrients it needs through their roots. However, don't think that dead wood is useless for the forest! On the contrary, many types of fungi and insects will use it for a long time to come.

Protection against the wind

The wind is useful, as it can carry small seeds hundreds of miles across the country. Sometimes, though, it goes crazy and blows up a storm. Then everything in its path goes flying. But can slender forest trees hold their ground? And how do they do it?

Can trees stop the wind?

Fortunately, all trees have **branches** that can withstand the wind (coniferous trees in particular are excellent at protecting the forest from the wind all year round). And when tall trees and low shrubs join forces, they stand a much better chance against the wind. **Shrubs** (such as rose, euonymus, blackberry, privet, and elderberry bushes) are excellent at protecting the forest against ground-level winds.

When a strong wind blows . . .

When the wind really picks up, it doesn't seem like a very good idea to linger around in the forest, right? You're much better off avoiding the falling trees and branches. But the truth is that a forest, which is made up of different kinds of trees, is the best landscape for withstanding strong gusts of wind. It's usually only the old and very dry trees that succumb to a gale . . .

The layers of the forest

In addition to trees and shrubs, the forest has a few other layers that provide a cosy retreat for large animals as well as small insects.

1. **Tree layer** – plants over 16 feet high
2. **Shrub layer** – plants reaching heights of between 3 and 16 feet
3. **Herb layer** – all woody and herbaceous plants under 3 feet
4. **Moss layer** – moss and lichen
5. **Root layer** – plant roots and fungi mycelium (a hidden network that helps brings life to the soil)

Forests on the move

Trees can't walk or run, right? Of course they can't. Luckily, they have seeds with wings and various fluffy coatings that are propelled by the wind or carried by animals. These fly across the world, spreading the legacy of their ancestors to places you might not expect.

Adventurous seeds

As we know, young trees primarily grow from seeds. The seeds of coniferous trees are hidden inside cones. In the warmth of the spring, these open up and the seeds fall to the ground and put down roots. Some of them take root right next to the parent trunk and grow under its protection, while others may travel on for several miles. But the greatest travelers among seeds come from some deciduous trees, namely birch and poplar.

How seeds travel around the world

With their delicate wings, **maple seeds** (1) simply drift down to the ground like miniature helicopters. **Willow** (2), **birch** (3), and **poplar** (4) seeds are covered in a light fluffy down and are carried much further by the wind. For example, a willow seed can fly up to 100 miles from its original home! And each willow can produce tens of millions of seeds.

We're flyyying!

Prepare for take-off!

Birches are true adventurers among trees. They can make themselves at home in places where no other trees are growing, particularly sunny meadows and the edges of forests – in the depths of the forest they lack the sunlight urgently needed for them to live. Unlike other types of trees, birches are independent and can happily fend for themselves without help from their parent trees. And because they are among the first to occupy unforested areas, they – along with willows, maples, and poplars – are called **pioneer** or **self-seeding trees**. When all these bold young trees get together, they are able to establish a forest even in treeless plains.

How long do trees live?

Although self-seeding trees grow at lightning speed, they have a very short life. Some of them only live up to 100 years – which is not a lot for a tree! Meanwhile, an oak or a redwood ages much more slowly, often taking as long as 2,000 years. Would you like to know the age of some of the world's oldest trees? Well, a long-lived Californian pine aptly named Methuselah is over 4,850 years old! This ancient can still recall the Stone Age, when our forebears lived mainly by hunting and gathering forest fruits. And believe it or not, there are even older trees. A Patagonian cypress in Chile's Alerce Costero National Park, for example, has reached the incredible age of 5,484!

Little homebodies

Some seeds are too heavy to be carried by the wind. Even so, they can still set off on a trip – in a squirrel's paws, a bird's beak, or hidden in a bear's fur … These animals like to collect seeds and carry them to secret hiding places. It might seem that these little homebodies, which include the hazelnut, could all too easily end up in someone's stomach … However, many seeds roll away during the journey or are forgotten about by the animal, who sometimes has more than one burrow and whose eyes are often bigger than their bellies.

The long journey north

And so, in all these different ways, entire forests are able to travel thanks to their light or heavy seeds … What are their preferred destinations? They prefer to head north. Can you guess why? It's because our planet is slowly getting warmer. So trees let their seeds fall a little further north each time, traveling at a speed of about 12 miles per century in search of cooler conditions. Although this is not exactly lightning fast, just imagine that within a century, the forest you can see from your window will have grown a few miles further north!

Let's experiment in the forest!

Have you ever tried sprouting your own seeds? All you have to do is bring seeds back from a trip to the forest and place them in a small dish on a damp piece of paper. It's important to keep it moist and give the seeds a light soaking from time to time.

Watch to see how many seeds germinate. Of course, you can sprout other seeds as well. You can even eat the sprouts of peas or lentils – they're a rich source of vitamins!

What's it like to have a fungus as a neighbor?

Have you ever noticed how well fungi grow when they're close to trees? And trees in the presence of fungi? Why is that? And what is behind it? The answer is little thing we call symbiosis – a relationship where two species help each other to benefit them both.

We fungi come from a strange kingdom somewhere between plants and animals. As you can see, we multiply by means of spores …

We are among the oldest organisms on Earth and we can live to a ripe old age!

SUGAR

I grow by the roots of trees, as a proper honey fungus should, and I sometimes steal a few nutrients from them. But hardly ever, I swear!

1. hoof fungus
2. common honey fungus
3. fly agaric
4. bay bolete
5. chanterelle

The oldest fungus in the world

The oldest known fungus in the world is an Armillaria ostoyae growing in the state of Oregon in the Pacific Northwest. Its **mycelium** covers an area of almost 4 square miles, which is bigger than 1,665 soccer fields! Scientists believe it is between 2,000 and 8,000 years old, making it both the oldest *and* largest organism in the world.

2 KM

Look – the mycelium of one fungus in Oregon stretches across this whole area!

A fragile friendship

Do you know why fungi like to grow so close to trees? It's because they help one another – that funny thing we call **symbiosis**. What form does this help take and when is it needed? For example, when the root connection that trees use to send important messages and nutrients to each other is suddenly broken (perhaps nibbled by a mouse or gouged out by a hungry boar). That's when the fungus comes into its own. Using the threads of its mycelium, it links the two ends of the broken root back together again, re-establishing communication between the trees. Some fungi can even protect the roots of their trees from other wood-destroying fungi or bacteria. However, they don't do this free of charge – each time they take some of the nutrients from the trees that they need for their own growth …

Fungi pirates

Some fungi are a bit like pirates – they take the tree's nutrients but give them nothing in return and can even make them ill. For example, sometimes a honey fungus will slowly and sneakily take away so much sugar from a nearby tree that it eventually becomes exhausted and dies.

The silent rulers of the forest kingdom

Fungi are very clever organisms that can outsmart other intelligent creatures such as ants. One Brazilian species is even able to grow right through the body of an unsuspecting ant if the poor thing accidentally swallows some of its spores …

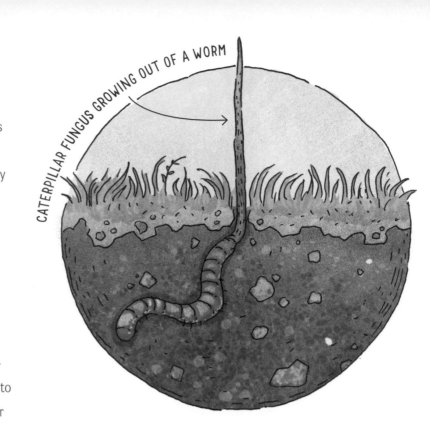

CATERPILLAR FUNGUS GROWING OUT OF A WORM

The caterpillar fungus behaves in a similar way and can grow out of a caterpillar, spider, or worm. Fortunately, there is balance in nature. As well as the fungi pirates, we also find gardener ants in the forest, which grow their own fungi. They have been feeding on them for millions of years, and during that time they even cultivated their own species of fungus!

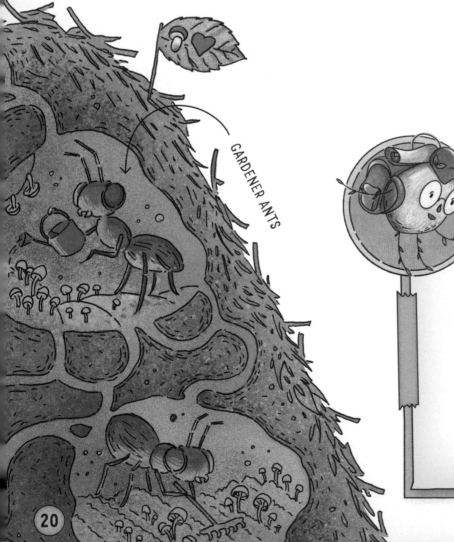

GARDENER ANTS

Let's experiment in the forest!

Play detective and track down fungus mycelium that can't be seen above the ground. How deep down do these mycelium go? If you're persistent enough, you might end up digging pretty deep … because a single mycelium can grow for many feet underground …

How do trees get along with ants?

The silent forest giants welcome some ants with open arms, while there are others they would rather run away from. That's the way of the world. So, what kind of relationship do trees and hardworking ants have? Who is a friend and who is more of a pest to the trees?

Ants as the first gardeners

Although some fungi can take control of ants, there is also a South American species of ant, the Atta ant, that actually grows fungus. They have colonies of up to ten million citizens – more than the entire population of London! The Atta ants tend their underground gardens, which are made out of leaves, twigs, and excrement, and they use this fertile soil to grow fungus, which they then feed on. Just imagine, they became gardeners 50–60 million years before we humans did.

Please, hurry up! We need more chambers for our fungi gardens.

Ants as animal breeders

Of course, ants can also damage trees. Especially farmer ants, who breed a tiny bug called aphids. The aphids extract sugar sap from the trees and then excrete it in the form of sweet honeydew, which the ants just can't get enough of. However, the aphids damage the trees by pricking holes in them and then sucking out the nutrients until the trees wither and die. Other ants breed the caterpillars of blue butterflies. They look after them like babies – during the day they take them out into the fresh air and at night they bring them back into the anthill to sleep. But this care and attention doesn't come for free – in exchange, the caterpillars provide the ants with a sweet secretion which they adore. ♥

Yum–yum, ant larvae are the most delicious treat!

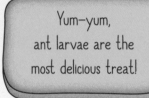

1. breeders
2. builders
3. suppliers
4. explorers
5. queen
6. eggs
7. larva

Hey, guys, who's going to help me carry this big leaf?

① ③ ②

Ants as tree defenders

On the other hand, even the most harmful ants can also help trees. They protect them against bark beetles, which attack trees and destroy their branches and trunks. How do these tiny little creatures do it? They simply trap the bark beetles and drag them back to the anthill, where they feed them to their larvae. These bark beetles provide vital nutrition for ant babies, which helps them to grow up big and strong. And that's not all! The industrious ants are wonderful forest cleaners, thoroughly clearing it of carrion (dead animal meat), which of course they also eat.

Ants as master builders

You've probably seen big anthill mounds in the forest. An ant community is very similar to a bee's. All the ants work together, and like bees, they also have a queen who establishes a new colony of ants. Ants can be found all around the world – from the desert to the polar regions.

Let's experiment in the forest!

Try to find different types of anthills in the forest – not just familiar mounds but also ant nests in tree hollows or in the crowns of trees. Can you find aphids there too? You can put out some breadcrumbs for the ants. Watch how they grapple with a piece of food two or three times their size – they're real musclemen!

Oh, the parasites!

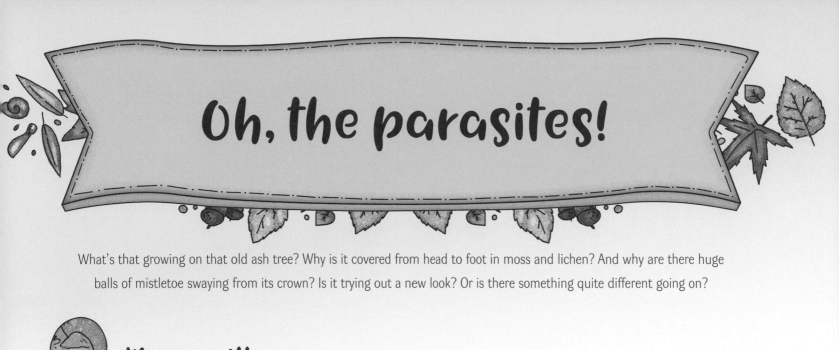

What's that growing on that old ash tree? Why is it covered from head to foot in moss and lichen? And why are there huge balls of mistletoe swaying from its crown? Is it trying out a new look? Or is there something quite different going on?

Mossy pillows

A forest isn't just made up of trees that are tall, welldeveloped, old, young, or very thin. In a forest you will also find moss at almost every turn. This plant is excellent at retaining water. If you touch moss shortly after it has rained, you will discover that it is full of water, just like a sponge. Moss likes dark, damp places, which is why it is so happy in the forest. Just imagine, it has been growing on Earth for hundreds of millions of years and there are around 20,000 species!

1. mistletoe (shrub)
2. beard lichen
3. common hair moss
4. cladonia (lichen)
5. tube lichen

Hi, who are you? You look a bit down ... What can I do for you?

Look, it's starting to rain! I'd better open my umbrella so I don't sprout here ...

Wow! I see a little water did you a world of good! Some like the sun and others prefer water!

Have you heard about lichen?

FUNGUS

ALGAE

LICHEN

At first sight it looks like moss, but it isn't. So what is it? Can you guess? Well, lichen is a unique organism made up of a community of **fungi** and **algae** or bacteria. In this book you've already read about the beneficial alliance called symbiosis. So, how does this work with lichen? The fungus provides the algae with water and shade, and in return the algae helps the fungus through photosynthesis, as fungi are unable to photosynthesize. Thanks to the algae's photosynthesis, the fungus is fed well and can thrive. And they call this common lichen.

With lichen to space and beyond...

Lichen is perhaps the **slowest growing organism on Earth** and is found practically everywhere – from the desert to the Himalayas to the icy Antarctic. Scientists have even discovered that lichen is so hardy it can survive in orbit in space! Despite the fact that it grows everywhere, lichen is in some ways quite picky. It is very **sensitive to air quality**; it turns its nose up at pollution and prefers to choose another place to grow. It doesn't have roots, so it doesn't need to take up water from the ground – it absorbs it with its whole surface. It is one of the pioneer species and, as we know, this means it is the first to grow in places where nothing else is growing.

Who or what is a parasite?

We've learned that in nature there are organisms which provide useful services to each other and live together in symbiosis. But what if someone is so sly that they only want to take without giving anything in exchange? We call this kind of relationship parasitic.

A **parasite** is an organism which takes advantage of its host without giving anything back. For example, after a walk in the forest you might find a tick in your arm or a flea in your dog's fur – these are parasites which live off our blood. And what do we get from them? A lot of itching is all!

Sneaky nutrient thieves

Lichen can also behave in a slightly parasitic way. It establishes itself on rotting wood or on rocks, or even on the bark or leaves of tropical trees, and then it disturbs them day after day. This creates a pathway for fungi and bacteria, which find it easy to get inside through the damaged surface. The branches of the afflicted tree slowly but surely start to wither. On the other hand, the destructive power of lichen helps dead trees to decompose much more quickly in the forest.

Deceptively beautiful mistletoe...

Like moss and lichen, mistletoe is also a parasite. These round bouquets, with their beautiful white berries, attach themselves to trees and unscrupulously steal their hard-earned nutrients, destroying them in the process. They are mainly found on deciduous trees such as lime, willow, hornbeam, poplar, and ash. Nevertheless, people like mistletoe and even decorate their homes with it at Christmastime.

Oh, the (animal) parasites!

These are bark beetles. These little beasts and their relatives attack us – ouch!

Anyone can be a parasite – not just mistletoe, moss, or lichen, but small animals too. Who would trees most like to avoid? Bark beetles, of course! And yet we shouldn't be too quick to condemn them. Even these voracious little beetles can be useful to the forest! Really? Really . . .

Those pesky bark beetles!

Bark beetles are tiny bugs that like to live beneath the bark of trees. They crawl right through it and their larvae chew little tunnels in it . . .

NORWAY SPRUCE

EUROPEAN SPRUCE BARK BEETLE

BARK BEETLE LARVAE

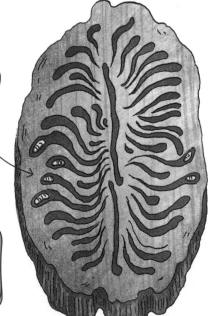

Yum, yum, spruce bark is my favorite!

What kind of bug is that?

WOODPECKER

BAT

Quick, grab it before an owl swoops in!

Bark beetles – tree eaters

Bark beetles feed on the **inner bark** of trees. Like our veins, the inner bark distributes the nutrients produced during photosynthesis around the body of the tree – from the green surfaces of the leaves all the way down to the roots. Apart from the European spruce bark beetle, other species of bark beetle live in forests in various parts of the world. They attack other trees – for example, American redwoods.

But don't go thinking that bark beetles are just villains and troublemakers. They mainly attack weak trees, which is (rightly or wrongly) the natural way of things. And trees are not totally powerless against them either. They are able to warn their tree friends about an imminent attack by these (at first sight) cute little bugs and launch a defense by releasing a **resin** that the bark beetles drown in. However, to do this, they must be healthy and strong.

Everything bad is good for something

Bark beetles love warm, dry conditions. When winters are mild and summers are hot and rain-free, many bark-beetle eggs survive and they go on to spread easily in single-species spruce forests.

However, the world isn't black and white, and everything bad is good for something. Just imagine, even bark beetles can help forests. In their own unique way, they are trying to **restore the natural multi-species forest**. Instead of there being nothing but conifers everywhere, they make room for beeches, oaks, maples and other trees. Unfortunately, they sometimes go about it a bit too enthusiastically … If people start planting different varieties of trees in the forest, they will also solve the bark-beetle problem.

Heeeeelp, a floooood!

RESIN

Woodpeckers

It's not just bark beetles that are happy to take advantage of what trees (willingly or not) provide them with – woodpeckers bore holes into trees so they can feast on … you've guessed it: bark beetles! However, trees are not exactly thrilled about these building projects – to them, each hole the woodpecker drills is an open wound that increases the risk of rotting … And as soon as the meal is over, the lovable woodpecker moves on to its banquet elsewhere.

Hollow trees

Trees are **home to many other animals**: owls, bats, martens, squirrels, nuthatches, and titmice. An old tree can almost look like a big hotel, where you can meet various neighbors passing through all its corridors. The squirrels, for example, are very talented builders. They can make cozy nests and warm them, even when it's extremely cold outside, up to a constant, pleasant temperature of 70 degrees Fahrenheit – which, by the way, is probably the same temperature you have in your room!

EAGLE OWL

Tree dwellers

1. wood nuthatch
2. great tit
3. stag beetle
4. fire salamander
5. pine marten
6. tawny owl
7. cross spider
8. red squirrel
9. honeybee
10. great spotted woodpecker
11. hoof fungus
12. red wood ant
13. European hedgehog
14. edible dormouse
15. common mole

Let's experiment in the forest!

Nowadays, especially near cities, it's difficult for birds to find a fully grown, preferably hollow tree to set up shop in. If you want to help them, you can build a home for them! It isn't hard to do. If you have a garden, the birds will reward you by gobbling up worms and slugs – a great tit, for example, can save up to 90% of a crop from them. Or you can just enjoy the singing of the birds and their playful flitting around outside your window.

HOLLOW TREE

Wow, there's a lot of you guys!

The secret kingdom beneath the tree roots

Treetops are teeming with life: birds singing on the branches, squirrels hiding in the hollows, not to mention the number of insects found on a tree! But what is it like down below … in the underground kingdom of the roots? Does anyone live there?

LAYERS OF LEAVES IN THE FALL

3 feet

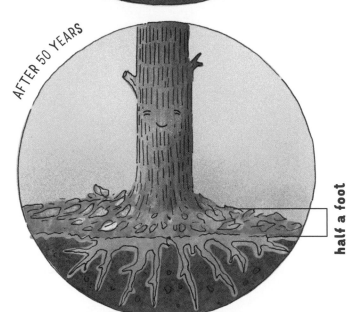

AFTER 50 YEARS

half a foot

Where do the fallen leaves go?

The forest floor is made up mostly of the leaves that most trees shed every autumn. However, before the trees shake off their bushy crowns, they transfer all the substances they no longer need into the leaves – just like us taking out the rubbish … Only then do the leaves let go of the branches and fall to the ground.

All of these fallen leaves slowly break down – or, more precisely, are broken down. They are helped out by **earthworms**, **beetles**, **woodlice**, **springtails**, and **fungi** … but also **mites** and **bacteria**. All of them feed on the remains of dead plants and animals, and they always gobble up a little dirt, excreting a fertile mash that we call **humus**. This is full of nutrients and minerals, allowing trees and other plants to grow at an astonishing rate! What's more, it only takes three years to prepare this nutritious treat, which is the blink of an eye in the life of a tree. The process of **decomposition** is not only important for the production of humus. Can you imagine if all the fallen leaves piled up through the ages? Before long you wouldn't even be able to see the top of the tallest tree through the heap!

Life in the soil

A whole mysterious world lies beneath the blanket of leaves! If we had a worm's-eye view, we would see a massive number of microorganisms living down there – mainly beside the roots, as that is where they can help themselves the most.

Fun fact: The woodlice that live in the soil usually have no eyes. Why? Well, because they don't need them for their underground life. It's pitch black down there, so tactile feelers are more useful.

Forest decomposition

1. fallen leaves

2. first level of decomposition – bacteria and fungi break down leaves into humus

3. second level of decomposition – springtails and roundworms feed on bacteria and fungi

4. third level of decomposition – earthworms, centipedes, and larger beetles feed on springtails and roundworms

5. nutrients from humus are absorbed by trees through roots

layers strongly affected by the weather

layers minimally affected by the weather

How many beetles can fit underground?

Just imagine, in an area the size of a dog's kennel there can be as many as 100,000 of these vitally important little creatures! If you look very closely, you might be able to spot beetles in the soil – but you'll have to look very carefully, because these springtails measure only a few millimeters.

1 POUND OF MICROORGANISM = 1 POUND OF NUTRIENTS FOR THE FOREST

PROTEIN

SUGAR   FAT

EARTHWORM VENTILATION SYSTEM: SUPPLYING THE FINEST OXYGEN DIRECTLY TO THE ROOTS

Helpful earthworms

Earthworms are curious little animals. They are social creatures that communicate by touch and breathe through the whole surface of their body. They help trees because the tunnels they dig in the soil loosen it and improve its quality. When it rains, the water is directed deep down beneath the tree, which can then draw moisture from it. It doesn't run off the surface, meaning that earthworms are excellent at preventing floods.

Rotting wood

Many beetles see green leaves and living wood as a tempting treat, as well as an excellent place to build a new home. Of course, it's much better if the beetles choose a fallen trunk or branch for their voracious larvae than a perfectly healthy tree that is still growing …

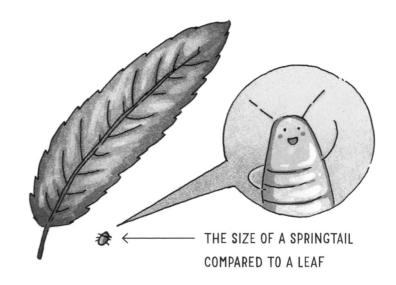

THE SIZE OF A SPRINGTAIL COMPARED TO A LEAF

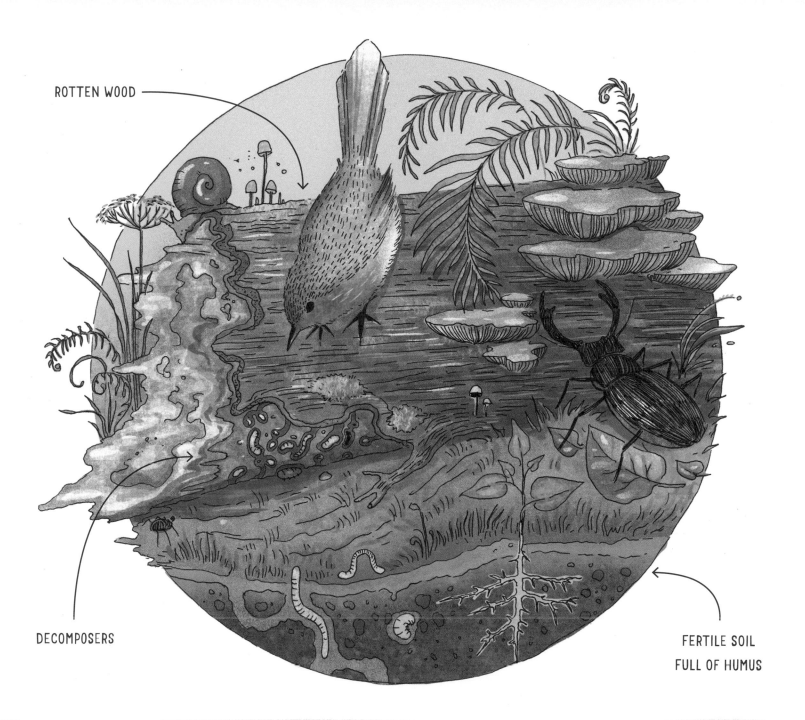

ROTTEN WOOD

DECOMPOSERS

FERTILE SOIL
FULL OF HUMUS

Is dead wood really dead?

If you crumble dead wood, you are left with loose soil between your fingers ... which is very important for **forest regeneration**. After many, many years, every tree rots, until all that is left of it is a mound of loose soil. This is why ancient forests, where dead trees are left to decompose naturally, are bumpy and full of hollows and mounds. The loose soil from dead trees is truly miraculous because absolutely everything thrives in it – seedlings, ferns, moss and lichen, insects, amphibians, reptiles, and even mammals.

Why do leaves fall in autumn?

Here comes autumn, the most colorful season of the year! It paints the leaves gold and bright red just before they fall to the ground, leaving the trees bare. But where do these beautiful colors come from? And why do trees get rid of their leaves?

Why are leaves so colorful in autumn?

Most of the time, deciduous trees are green thanks to a **green pigment called chlorophyll**, and also because of photosynthesis, which highlights this pigment in the leaves. However, as summer comes to an end, the sunlight fades and so the chlorophyll starts to break down, causing the leaves to slowly lose their green color. This makes the remaining colors stand out all the more!

How can trees transform themselves like that?

SUMMER – THE GREEN PIGMENT CHLOROPHYLL CATCHES THE SUN'S RAYS

AUTUMN – THE LEAVES HIGHLIGHT OTHER DIFFERENT COLORS

Why do leaves fall?

Trees take a nap in winter, so they don't need as much nutrition then as in the spring, when they produce blossoms, or in the hot summer when their fruit ripens. They shed their old leaves because without them it is easier to conserve water during the cold season. What's more, if trees drank too much before winter, their branches would be full of water and would easily snap during a frost.

DRAWING WATER FROM THE
GROUND IN SPRINGTIME

AUTUMNAL REST

A TYPICAL MATURE TREE CAN CONTAIN 100–250 GALLONS OF WATER IN THE SUMMER. THAT'S THE
SAME AS 3–6 FULL BATHTUBS! IN AUTUMN THIS AMOUNT IS REDUCED TO ABOUT HALF.

What about conifers?

While deciduous trees welcome the winter with bare branches, conifers remain covered with lots of **needles**. Do their needles ever fall off? Appearances can be deceiving. In reality their needles also fall off, but never all at once. Each winter, they keep their needles from several previous years.

I change my needles once every three years!

PINE

It takes me five years, but I'm not going anywhere in a hurry.

SPRUCE

We conifers often grow in colder areas and in the mountains, so we are well prepared for snow and ice. We don't have to go into hibernation like deciduous trees, and then in the spring we don't have to waste time renewing all of our needles. In short, we've got it all figured out!

FIR

Thin but tough pine needles

Pine needles have a smaller surface area than leaves, so less water evaporates from them. Moreover, coniferous trees can mix saved water with sugar and make antifreeze syrup. Most pine needles also have a special protective layer against frost!

DECIDUOUS LARCH
I'm a larch and although I am a conifer ... I lose all my needles in wintertime

I grow in places like the Russian taiga (far northern forests) and I am used to really harsh, long winters ... but I can't make antifreeze syrup.

So if I kept my needles all winter, I would be terribly thirsty because of the water that would evaporate from them ...

How wolves saved the forest

You already know that even bark beetles, which people get very annoyed about, can be beneficial for the forest. But have you ever thought about wolves? How do these predators affect life in their habitat? In Yellowstone National Park in the USA they know a thing or two about it: there was a time when wolves had completely disappeared from the park and local nature was in a sorry state …

In Yellowstone National Park

A long time ago, Yellowstone used to be full of wolves. However, the local farmers were worried about their animals, and so they hired hunters who hunted the wolves until there were none left. In the 1920s, there wasn't a wolf hair to be found in Yellowstone.

And because all the animals and plants in the forest (and in nature in general) are bound together by a mysterious invisible network, the trees and animals along the riverbanks disappeared along with the wolves.

DOUGLAS FIR

They were tough times … But you want to know if life ever returned to Yellowstone, right?

YELLOWSTONE AROUND 1930

What happened to the trees?

When the wolves disappeared, the number of deer increased, and they feasted on young willows and poplars. Without the roots of these trees, the water began to spill out into the surrounding area. In time, however, the sun dried it up and this parched earth slowly began to crack and erode until almost no plants could live there. The shade that had kept beavers and frogs cool vanished along with the plants, and there were hardly any branches left for the birds. And so, together with the wolves, a precious piece of nature slowly disappeared.

GREY WOLF

Don't worry, I'll take care of you!

Wolves are **shy animals** that live in packs whose members look after each other. If a wolf is sick or injured, the other members of the pack will look after it for as long as a whole year.

How the wolves restored balance

Yellowstone National Park changed beyond recognition. Fortunately, the wolves returned to the park in 1995. They immediately set about hunting the numerous deer. As a result, the deer began to move more and they spent less time near watercourses where the wolves hunted. After many decades, the willows, aspens and poplars started to grow because the deer couldn't eat them all. Beaver and trout returned to the rivers and the number of birds increased. Many wetlands and pools were created which became a paradise for amphibians … And so the wolves brought life back to Yellowstone and transformed it into a functioning ecosystem once more.

1. Wapiti: How come there's more and more of us but the land is failing … ?

2. Doe: I'm afraid there might be too many of us …

3. Wolf: There's no need to be so afraid of me. I mainly hunt sick and weak creatures which could infect other animals. I usually avoid people …

4. Grizzly bear: I'm a bit wary when it comes to wolves, but they do make good neighbours. With fewer deer there are more berries for me.

5. Bald eagle: I love tidying up what the wolves leave behind. Not a scrap goes to waste!

6. Marmot: Where are the coyotes? Hurrah, there are hardly any of them!

7. Hawk: But the number of voles has increased!

8. Beaver: I haven't seen so many kinds of trees in years! I wonder which bark tastes the best?

9) Boreal chorus frog: Maybe I've eaten too many mosquitos …

10) Cutthroat trout: I like the purest mountain streams with a lot of oxygen.

YELLOWSTONE 60 YEARS LATER

41

Not all forests are the same: Types of forests

Forests make up close to a third of our planet's surface and there are about three trillion trees growing in them …
It's obvious that Australian forests look completely different from, say, Siberian forests. So what types of forests
are there? And where are they all found?

TYPES OF FOREST

TAIGA

MIXED FOREST

TROPICAL FOREST

MANGROVES

SISKIN

The higher up
a forest lies, the colder
it is there … Look!

Siskin – an agile little bird that can climb and even hang
upside down while searching for food. Oh, the things it'll do to
get ahold of some insects and seeds! It mainly lives in Europe
and East Asia, and high up in the branches of conifers it
builds its nests out of twigs, grass, moss, and lichen.

Under a different sky, a different forest

In various parts of the world you'll find different types of forests … That's because they each grow in a different climate. **Climate** refers to the usual weather in a particular area … It simply means how hot or cold it is in a particular place and how much it rains there. Both of these things have to do with its distance from the equator. For example, the sun's rays don't have far to go to the tropical rainforest, which is why it's hot there. But it also depends on how high up a forest lies – if it rises up high into the mountains, it's cooler there. Over the years, **animals and plants in these forests have adapted to these conditions**.

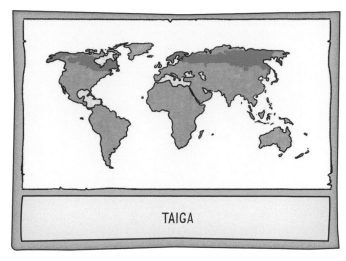

TAIGA

Taiga – the winter forest

Forests in the north of Europe, America, and Asia are called taiga. And this is no place for the faint of heart – winter in the taiga is really harsh! But it suits hardy animals like reindeer, Arctic hares, and foxes, as well as trees like spruce, fir, and pine. The ground is covered with a magnificient carpet of green moss!

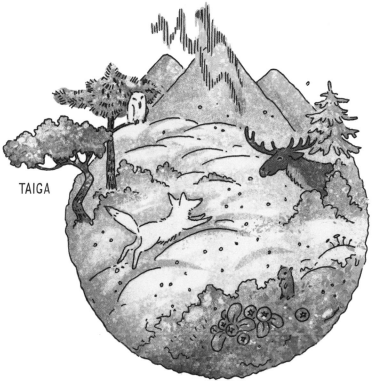

TAIGA

Quaking aspens are my favorite breakfast!

PANDO

Pando: The heaviest living organism

Pando is a super fascinating organism. It weighs over 6,000 tons – that's about the same as a thousand elephants! Growing in a mixed forest in Utah, it's not a single tree but a **giant colony of quaking aspen** stems that share a **single root system** … They're basically like identical twin trees. In recent years, however, they've been losing weight, mainly because deer and other animals have been munching on them.

MIXED FOREST

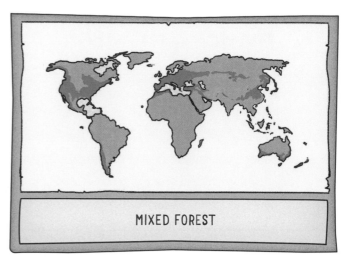

Mixed forest

Mixed forests mostly grow in the middle zone, where there are four distinct seasons and plenty of rainfall. Beech, oak, hornbeam, and maple trees do particularly well in them. However, you will also find conifers such as fir, pine, larch, and spruce. And the wildlife includes squirrels, hares, foxes, lynxes, badgers, wolves, and bears – in short, excellent animal company! But lots of mixed forests have been cut down on a large scale and turned into pure spruce forests, which are used for timber.

MANGROVES

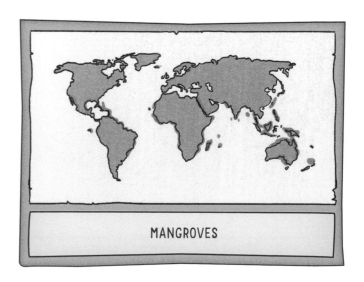

MANGROVES

Mangroves – when water meets land

In the tropics, there are forests growing on the coast and in river deltas that are called mangroves, where freshwater mixes with saltwater. This is a community of trees and shrubs that are noticeable for their roots. Lounging among them are anemones, fish, starfish, crocodiles, herons, and pelicans. Because of this, the seeds of some mangrove trees prefer to do their sprouting up in the tree and only let go once they are ready to latch on to the soil; otherwise, they could be washed away by the current or eaten by animals. And imagine how brave mangroves are! They are able to stand up to a tsunami wave and soften its impact.

TROPICAL RAINFOREST

Tropical rainforest

The tropical rainforest is home to an almost incalculable number of species. These are very dense forests – the trees grow close to each other with their branches intertwining. There can be as many as 950 species of beetle living on a single tree! In addition to them, you can spot various monkeys, snakes, frogs, and lizards in the branches.

CONGOLIAN RAINFOREST

INDONESIAN RAINFOREST

The forest water cycle

Has it ever occured to you that the forest is full of water? No doubt you'll immediately picture springs, babbling brooks, and fast-flowing torrents … But there's water in other parts of the forest too – you just might not notice it at first glance …

It soaks up water and holds onto it

Freshwater around the world is getting scarcer … If things continue like this, many lakes and watercourses will dry up soon. Moss can hold a lot of water, and in heavy rain it can increase its size up to ten times! And if there is only light rain, trees can absorb a third of the rainwater. But what if not a single drop falls … ? Or, on the contrary, what if a huge amount falls in a short time? Then it's only the roots that can help, as they can slow the rate at which rivers flow or dry up for a time.

Yaaay, water! I feel happy in it!

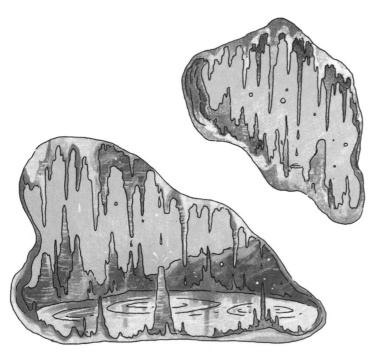

Underground water

The forest soil itself holds some water, but only if it has a deep and dense enough network of roots and it is regularly loosened by earthworms. In that case, there's less danger of **erosion** – i.e., of the soil being washed away by the rain. This is every forest's nightmare … The water, which is filtered down through the roots, down to where the soil gives way to rock, can carve out tunnels or **cave systems** in even the hardest stone. These then become **reservoirs of clean underground water**, which sometimes returns to the surface in the form of gurgling streams or gushing springs.

The forest cleans water

The forest acts as a giant filter which gradually cleans water. First of all, **raindrops** pass through the leaves and branches of trees, then through bushes, herbs and moss, and finally they seep through the soil – there, thanks to the roots, the dirty rainwater is transformed into **pure water**.

Steam rises through the forest

It feels pleasant in a forest even when it is swelteringly hot and muggy all around. That's because on hot days the water from the entire forest evaporates, cooling the air inside it. We can often see **water vapor** rising upwards in the form of tiny droplets, which then turn into clouds and finally into rain.

THE CLOUDS TURN INTO HEAVY RAIN CLOUDS

... IT'S RAINING! THE RAIN SOAKS INTO THE SOIL ...

UNDERGROUND WATER SPOUTS UP AND EVAPORATES

Let's experiment in the forest!

You can find a large number of springs in the forest. However, before you drink from them, look for an information panel, which will tell you if the water is drinkable. In the springtime, you can help these springs by removing fallen leaves and other debris from them. Then the water will be lovely and clear!

Tropical rainforests

Welcome to the magical world of tropical rainforests – a world of colorful plants, towering trees, climbing lianas, and mysterious creatures. The day has ended and the rainforest has come alive with pollinators going about their work on the night shift, fruit bats flying out of their hiding places, and geckos scampering along branches with pythons hissing above … And that's what the rainforest is like night after night.

Wooow, that's beautiful! A nocturnal carnival. And so many animals!

It can get pretty wild here. They even say that two-thirds of all plant and animal species live here …

We all depend on each other, so we have to get along. The jungle needs all of its plants and animals …

Why are rainforests so important?

Tropical rainforests encircle the Earth like a belt around its center near the equator. The most extensive rainforest is found in the Amazon in South America, but we also find tropical jungles in Africa and Asia. It is always **humid** and **hot** there, which makes it perfect for an **enormous number of animals and plants**. You might even know some of them from your house, for example Swiss cheese plants.

Rainforests are gigantic reservoirs. It rains here several times a day.

The jungle as storage space

Tropical rainforests also contain enormous stores of carbon dioxide – a gas that neither people nor animals can breathe. When people cut down the rainforests, carbon dioxide is released into the atmosphere, adding to the dangerous ongoing **warming of the whole planet**. What a terrible thought! Which is why we have to **protect and cherish** the rainforests.

Healing forests

The rainforests are also home to **many indigenous tribes – people** who live in harmony with nature, who know all about the herbs of the jungle and can use them to treat even very serious illnesses. After all, almost half of the medicines people use originally come from the rainforest. That's why rainforests are sometimes called the **"green pharmacies of the world"**!

An experiment! How to protect the rainforests

Why do people cut down the rainforests? It's mostly so they can plant **palm trees** and use their fruit to make **palm oil**. But when the plantation has been cleared, all that is left is a bare, empty strip of land in place of the lush forest that is sadly now gone. Do you want to know one very simple way to help save the rainforests? Read the packaging of chocolate bars, chips, and other goodies, and if they contain palm oil, swap them for something that doesn't. The rainforests of the world will thank you for it!

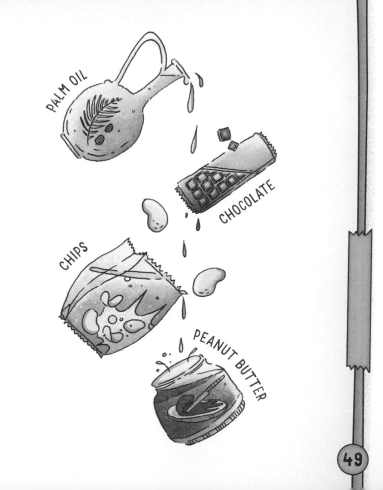

PALM OIL

CHOCOLATE

CHIPS

PEANUT BUTTER

1. Brazil nut: I'm one of the tallest trees in the Amazon. If the bee is able to pollinate my flower, it will develop into a tasty nut. The only problem is that only one type of bee can pollinate me. Their lives, in turn, are dependent on the magnificent local orchids ... Oh, this world is so complicated!

2. A bee pollinating an orchid: Oooh, an orchid! And hey there, a Brazil nut!

3. Hummingbird: I know how to fly forwards and backwards. Best of all, though, is that I can hover in one place ...

4. Three-toed sloth: Life in the jungle passes so s-l-o-o-o-w-l-y ...

5. Agouti: Ha-ha, no one will find these seeds!

6. Brazil nut seed: Keep us nice and warm. After we germinate, we'll grow up to be young Brazil nut trees – I can't wait!

7. Poison dart frog: If you were thinking of trying to eat me, I'd strongly recommend against it. I may be a beautiful color, but I'm very poisonous ...

8. Titan beetle: I'm the largest of all known beetles – I can grow up to half a foot long!

9. Jaguar: Most cats don't like swimming, but I'm an exception. I love hunting in the still night water, and at other times I'll climb high into the treetops.

10. Banana tree: Some unnamed purple orchids complain that I cast a shadow over them here in the rainforest and they can't grow! But what am I to do?

11. Black-headed spider monkey: A long tail always comes in handy when moving around branches!

12. Morpho butterfly: My brilliant blue wings change their shade according to the temperature.

13. Toco toucan: I always choose the most beautiful fruit for my female partner.

14. Giant anaconda: As one of the largest snakes, I weigh a whopping 220 pounds – can you believe it?

15. Scarlet macaw: *Craaahh!* You can hear me a mile away.

16. Red-eyed tree frog: My superpower is that I can change color based on my mood!

Does fire belong in the forest?

If you were to say the words "forest fire," everyone would immediately get ready to run. Because fire doesn't belong in a forest ... Or does it? Some trees wouldn't grow at all without fire. So, what is the truth about forest fires? For example, in Australia, fires are relatively frequent. They can be caused by lightning or volcanoes, or sometimes the trees catch fire even by themselves in the heat ...

Fire-loving trees

However, this is good news for the **eucalyptus** and the **Australian banksia**. Their seeds are enclosed within tight capsules and will only come out in extreme heat – for example, during a fire. Then the capsules open up and the seeds have a chance to grow in the fertile ash-rich soil. These two strange species of tree then **rise like a phoenix from the ashes**! For trees that aren't used to fire, however, a forest fire can spell disaster. All you need is one badly put-out campfire or a piece of glass that acts like a magnifying glass and all hell can break loose. Deciduous trees can resist fire a little longer, but for dry spruce trees all it takes is one little spark and because of their resin they go up like match-

es. The resulting fire can spread through a forest at speeds of up to 100 miles per hour – which is why we should only make fires in designated areas and always extinguish them properly.

Save yourselves!

Fire is also dangerous for animals. In Australian forests, the unfortunate fleeing animals can be saved by **wombat burrows**. Wombats are marsupials that look a bit like hairy pigs. They like to dig vast networks of underground burrows, where other animals – such as insects, reptiles, and birds, as well as koalas, echidnas (egg-laying mammals also called spiny anteaters), and even kangaroos – can take shelter.

1. Kangaroo family: I think we have a chance of escaping! We can jump distances over 30 feet!

2. Koala: Wombat, can I come into your burrow, please? I'm your closest living relative ...

3. Possum: H-e-e-l-p, fire! We have to move to another forest!

4. Cockatoo: Crrraa! Oh no, my tree hollow!

5. Termite: Fire? Oh no, and I'm photophobic – I'm sensitive to light! I'm afraid that my nest of dung and dirt has burned to the ground ...

6. Australian emperor moth: Is it just me or can my antennae detect smoke ...?

7. Stick insect: Now is probably not the time to disguise myself as a twig ...

8. Wombat: Everyone, quick, take shelter in the wombat burrows!

9. Eucalyptus: Where's everyone running off to? It's quite pleasant here ... I don't mind a little fire, and my seeds really like it. Straight away they'll have fertile soil to sprout in!

10. Banksia: Another hour at 280 degrees Fahrenheit and my seeds will pop out.

11. Banksia seed: Ahh, at last! The capsule has opened and I can jump out!

Who lives in the swamp?

If you find a swamp in a forest – at first sight a dirty and stinky bog – don't turn your nose up at it! It might not look like much, but it is incredibly important for the forest and its wildlife. For example, it can be used as a shelter from predators, as a source of sustenance, or as a water supply. Let's take a closer look …

What is a swamp?

Do you know how swamps – those small but really deep pools of dark water – are made? Well, it happens when it rains and rains until a large puddle forms. Over time, leaves get blown into it, insects get trapped in it, the odd frog jumps in … and then bacteria and algae gradually turn the clear water cloudy and it changes color from clear to pitch black.

The forest cleaner

However, a dark swamp like this is incredibly important, as it retains water in the forest. Like a huge sponge, it can absorb a large amount of water, which helps prevent flooding. It also acts as a natural filter – it cleans the water of chemicals released into it by thoughtless visitors.

1. Beaver: *Yaaay!* Another tree has fallen over there! Ideal material for building one of our grand dams and lodges.

2. Eurasian penduline tit: I prefer to make my nest out of nettle stalks and fluffy willow seeds.

3. Duck: Friends, I've found the perfect way to stay dry in wetlands – all you have to do is grease your feathers!

4. Carp: I'll swim down to take a look at the bottom. Maybe I'll dig out a worm or a tasty insect larva.

5. Frog: Nothing much happening today. Some days I can jump as far as three feet!

6. Heron: You see my thin neck and long legs? Thanks to them, I can dive really deep down chasing a fish.

7. Dragonfly: *Frrr!* Flies and mosquitoes beware – I'm an insect hunter and I'm on the lookout for a hearty dinner!

8. Turtle: I'm in no danger – I can hide in my shell from all those hungry mouths! The only one I don't want to spot me is the heron …

9. Lobster: Phew, who needs fishing poles? There's nothing quite like my pinchers. No fish can escape them!

Life in the swamp

For many plants and animals, swamps are a cosy home – literally the **source of life**. Plants that need to grow in permanently waterlogged soil thrive in them. In return, they provide sustenance and shelter for beautiful species of insects and other creatures: fish, crayfish and frogs as well as long-legged herons and cranes. They are perfectly hidden from predators among the thick stems and can also feast on the juicy stalks. In short, life in a swamp is just great!

A lure for birds

Unfortunately, there are not many proper swamps in the world … And that's a great shame, because wherever you find swamps, wetlands or pools, you will also find **large numbers of insects** – the greatest delicacy for birds. And scientists recently discovered something which birds have known for a very long time: that a kind of insect chimney forms above every swamp, a tunnel containing 25 times more insects than anywhere else. If people want more birds in the forest, then they will have to start by bringing back the forest swamps and pools …

Born in water, but living on land!

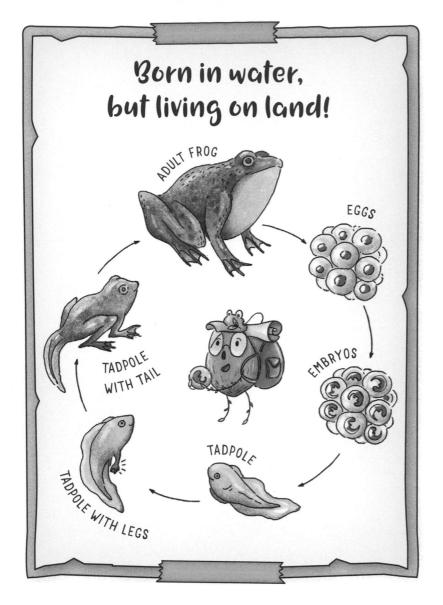

ADULT FROG

EGGS

EMBRYOS

TADPOLE

TADPOLE WITH LEGS

TADPOLE WITH TAIL

FRESHWATER MARSHES LAY BESIDE FOREST RIVERS OR LAKES, WHILE SALTWATER MARSHES LAY BESIDE THE COAST.

Frogs – synchronized swimmers

The whirring of dragonflies, the croaking of frogs, a constant sound of chirping … The frogs are especially fascinating! The diversity is incredible: the smallest frog, the Paedophryne amauensis from Papua New Guinea in the South Pacific, is less than half an inch long, while the biggest is the goliath frog from Cameroon at over one foot long. And the way they move! Even people try to imitate the frog's faultless swimming style.

A hop, skip, and a jump!

Did you know that the record long jump by a frog on land is a whopping 16 feet?! There's really nothing to it – all you need are very long, strong back legs … As well as being world champions at the long jump and being a great delicacy for the elegant herons, frogs are also very funny eaters. If you ever have the chance to watch a frog eating, you'll notice that it blinks all the time. But it's not doing it for fun! By retracting its eyeballs, the frog makes it easier for the food to go down into its belly …

The largest swamp in the world

One of the world's most spectacular swamps is located in the Pantanal National Park in Brazil and covers about 75,000 square miles. The swamp is created during the rainy season when the Paraguay River floods a large area of the western part of Brazil. And because the surrounding area is as flat as the bottom of a giant swimming pool, the water spreads out very easily.

Why do we need wood?

Every tree starts out as a small, modest seed. The trees grow tall and the day comes when some of them are cut down. This is because wood is an important material for people, which we have been using to make just about everything since ancient times …

A WOODCUTTER AND HIS DRAFT HORSE CAREFULLY TRANSPORT WOOD

LARGE-SCALE LOGGING WITH A HEAVY HARVESTER IS NOT PARTICULARLY KIND TO THE FOREST …

Trees and people

Wood has played a part in people's lives since prehistoric times. Even mammoth hunters made their first bows and arrows from wood, while people today have entire homes built from it. It is pleasantly **soft** but at the same time **strong**, and it also **smells good** … And even if we were to spend a thousand years looking for a substitute, we might never find a more perfect material. Wood is essential for humans … Plus, you can reuse it again and again or **recycle** it.

How wood is harvested

In the past, people had to work really hard to cut down trees. They had to cut them down with their bare hands using **hand-sharpened axes** and then drag them to the forest track with the **help of horses**. From there, they were taken to the sawmill, where the individual trunks were cut into planks, logs, and smaller pieces. Today, all you have to do is press a button on a chainsaw or make yourself comfortable in a harvester that does all the hard work for you … The only disadvantage is that in the forest, a giant like a harvester is like a bull in a china shop …

The destructive harvester

They can wreak havoc in the forest … These logging machines, weighing several tons, can sink into the ground to a depth of 7 feet as if it were nothing. After an earthquake like that, the poor little creatures in the soil are suddenly nowhere to be found. What's more, this kind of **heavy machinery presses down the soil**, compacting it. And because it's hard for this compacted earth to absorb water, no forest plants can thrive in or around it. All that remains are deep puddles full of standing water in rutted clearings.

DID YOU KNOW THAT TREES ARE AN IMPORTANT PART OF THIS BOOK TOO? ITS PAGES ARE MADE OF PAPER, WHICH CONTAINS WOOD. WHAT OTHER WOODEN THINGS DO YOU USE?

Think twice before cutting wood …

The wood from trees grows really s-l-o-o-w-l-y … Which is why **we shouldn't waste it**. It's OK to take a few logs from the forest to make a fire. But for every tree we cut down, **we should give back to the forest for its loss**.

Let's experiment in the forest!

Look around your bedroom and try to find a piece of wood. Notice its beautiful texture, smell, and temperature, and listen to the nice sound it makes when you tap it with your finger …

Things made of wood

1. the floor (oak)
2. wooden crates
3. a cello (spruce)
4. wooden building blocks
5. a stool made from a tree stump
6. a basket (willow wicker)
7. logs for a fire
8. a footbridge over a stream
9. a birdhouse
10. a coat stand made from branches
11. books

Visiting the forest

The forest is a place just made for relaxation. The rustle and fragrance of the trees, the birdsong, the pleasant crackle of fallen pine needles underfoot, the soft moss … All you have to do is lie back and take in all the beauty around you. Be careful, though – it's important to look after and cherish our forests, so every visit has to have its rules!

Yaaay, I feel as if the time has come … to put down roots in this beautiful and well-tended forest!

Let's experimentt in the forest!

Maybe you're thinking, who wouldn't want to settle down permanently in a forest? But for that, you would need a house … or would you? Try to imagine your own little forest home and then build either a small one or a large one. How should you go about it? Find a quiet place in a forest that you like, collect suitable materials – for example, branches, stones, or leaves – and then let your imagination guide you.

How to protect the forest at every step

TO AVOID AWAKENING THE ANIMALS FROM THEIR FOREST SLEEP, YOU SHOULD ALWAYS FOLLOW MARKED TRAILS IN THE FOREST AND NOT VEER OFF TRAIL.

YOU SHOULD ONLY TAKE AS MANY BLUEBERRIES, RASPBERRIES, OR OTHER GOODIES FROM THE FOREST AS YOU YOURSELF CAN EAT.

WALKING BAREFOOT THROUGH A FOREST WILL IMMEDIATELY IMPROVE YOUR MOOD. IT DOESN'T DISTURB THE FOREST WILDLIFE OR PREVENT SMALL SEEDS FROM GROWING.

SNACK WRAPPERS AND OTHER TRASH SHOULD BE THROWN AWAY ONCE YOU'RE BACK HOME. THIS IS THE ONLY WAY TO KEEP OUR FORESTS HEALTHY AND CLEAN!

A brief glossary of the forest

Chlorophyll – A green pigment in plants or the green color in leaves; it plays a very important part in photosynthesis (p. 36).

Decomposers – Tiny or microscopic animals, fungi, and bacteria that do invisible but vital work; they gradually break down leaves and dead animals into a fertile mixture called humus, which enriches the soil (pp. 27, 32, 33, 36).

Forest – A mysterious community of trees and other woodland plants, animals, and fungi that live together in close-knit relationships. They can help but sometimes also harm each other. There are many types of forest: boreal forest, taiga, mixed forest, tropical rainforest, watery mangroves, etc. (pp. 42, 43, 44, 45).

Fungus – A strange organism, neither plant nor animal. Fungi have their own separate kingdom and multiply through their spores or a network of fine roots (pp. 17, 18, 19, 20, 21, 24, 26, 32, 33).

Growth rings – Each year a tree gains one more growth ring. You might notice them on a cross section of a tree stump. An experienced woodsman can tell a lot from these rings (p. 10).

Harvester – A heavy machine designed to quickly cut down trees, lop off branches, and saw and stack wood from the forest (pp. 57, 58).

Hollow tree – Usually an old tree with lots of cavities and holes where birds and other forest animals often reside (pp. 30, 31).

Humus – A fertile layer of soil made up of the dead and decomposed remains of plants, animals, and fungi (pp. 32, 33, 35, 53).

Inner bark – A nutrient network directly below the outer bark of trees. Like our veins, the veins of inner bark act as a pipeline for a life-giving fluid known as sap, which is made up of water, sugars, proteins, minerals, and other substances (pp. 10, 28, 29).

Lichen – Another curious forest dweller – neither algae nor fungus but something in between. Lichen are among the oldest organisms on Earth (pp. 13, 25, 26, 27, 35, 42).

Mangroves – Communities of trees growing directly in water (even saltwater). Mangroves have thick roots, and swimming freely among them are small fish hunted by various aquatic birds (pp. 42, 44, 45).

Mixed forest – A forest with both deciduous and coniferous trees. They are mostly found in the temperate zone (pp. 42, 43, 44).

Monoculture – A forest planted with only one species of tree (such as spruce) so that people can harvest wood from it quickly and easy. However, this dense planting of trees with thin branches and shallow roots has many disadvantages (pp. 11, 29).

Moss – A tiny plant that forms a soft carpet wherever it's even a little damp and shady – so especially in the forest! (pp. 13, 25, 26, 27, 35, 42, 43, 46, 47)

Palm oil – A seemingly cheap oil that comes from the fruits of the oil palm tree. However, we pay dearly for its low price with more carbon dioxide in the atmosphere, because palm-oil plantations are mainly grown on fertile land created by cutting down vast swathes of tropical rainforests … (p. 49).

Paper – The paper in this book was also produced from a mixture of wood pulp (cellulose), recycled old paper, and a few other substances (pp. 58, 59).

Parasite – An animal, fungus, or plant that feeds by taking nutrients from other inhabitants of the forest (pp. 11, 25, 26, 27, 28, 29, 30).

Photosynthesis – A mysterious process inside the green leaves of a plant where water and carbon dioxide breathed in by the plant are turned into sugar through the effect of sunlight and warmth. Photosynthesis is hugely important for life on Earth – it's why we have enough oxygen and can breathe freely. (pp. 6, 7, 26, 29, 36).

Pioneer species – Adventurous trees or shrubs that may venture far away from their parent tree as tiny airborne seeds and eventually sprout in places where no other woody plants are growing (pp. 15, 27).

Pollinators – Animals that help plants to transfer pollen from their stamens to their pistils and thus to reproduce. As well as the busy bees and other insects, they also include butterflies, geckos, and even some small mammals (pp. 2, 3, 4, 5, 48, 50, 51).

Recycling – A process in which we reuse material we would otherwise throw in the trash (for example, we can make beautifully clean and new paper from old, scribbled paper thrown into a special container). This means that the original paper doesn't go to waste (p. 57).

Resin – A sticky fluid excreted mainly by coniferous trees when something or someone injures them (the resin helps to seal over the wound) or so that they can get rid of bothersome bark beetles or other parasites that want to hold a banquet in their wood (pp. 29, 53).

Seed – The embryo of a new life concealed within the fruit of each tree. Some seeds have a fluffy coating or wings. This allows the wind to easily carry them or they can gently float down to the ground by themselves. Others might be hidden, for example, within a nut (pp. 2, 3, 8, 14, 15, 16, 45, 50, 52, 53, 54, 60, 61).

Seedling – A sprouted seed with its first new leaves (pp. 3, 35).

Self-pollinating plants – Not all plants need help from pollinators or wind to pollinate. Some just pollinate themselves by transferring their own pollen (p. 3).

Soil erosion – An unwelcome process in which the forest soil gradually breaks down and is carried away by water or wind. This can be caused by logging machines called harvesters or by trees of only one species with shallow roots being grown (pp. 46, 58).

Symbiosis – A mutually beneficial relationship between two or more forest organisms that help one another (for example, ants feed aphids and get drops of honeydew from them in return) (pp. 2, 3, 4, 5, 8, 9, 19, 24, 26, 27, 33, 34, 39, 40, 41).

Taiga – A coniferous forest that grows chiefly in the north (for example, in Canada or Siberia) (pp. 42, 43).

Tree – A perennial plant (i.e., a plant that lives for more than two years) with a wooden stem (trunk) whose surface is often protected with bark. It can have leaves (deciduous trees) or fine needles (coniferous trees) growing from the branches of its crown.

Tropical rainforest – A type of forest found mostly in warm, wet regions. This lush tree cover is home to many rare species of plants and animals, and some parts of it are so inaccessible that there are even species we still don't know about. (pp. 5, 27, 42, 43, 45, 48, 49, 50, 51).

Scan the QR code for more
information and sources.

© B4U Publishing for Albatros,
an imprint of Albatros Media Group, 2024
5. května 1746/22, Prague 4, Czech Republic
Written by Klára Holíková, Ivi Niesner, and Jana Sedláčková
Illustrations © Katarina Kratochvílová
Translated by Graeme Dibble
Edited by Scott Alexander Jones

Printed in China by Leo Paper Group
www.albatrosbooks.com

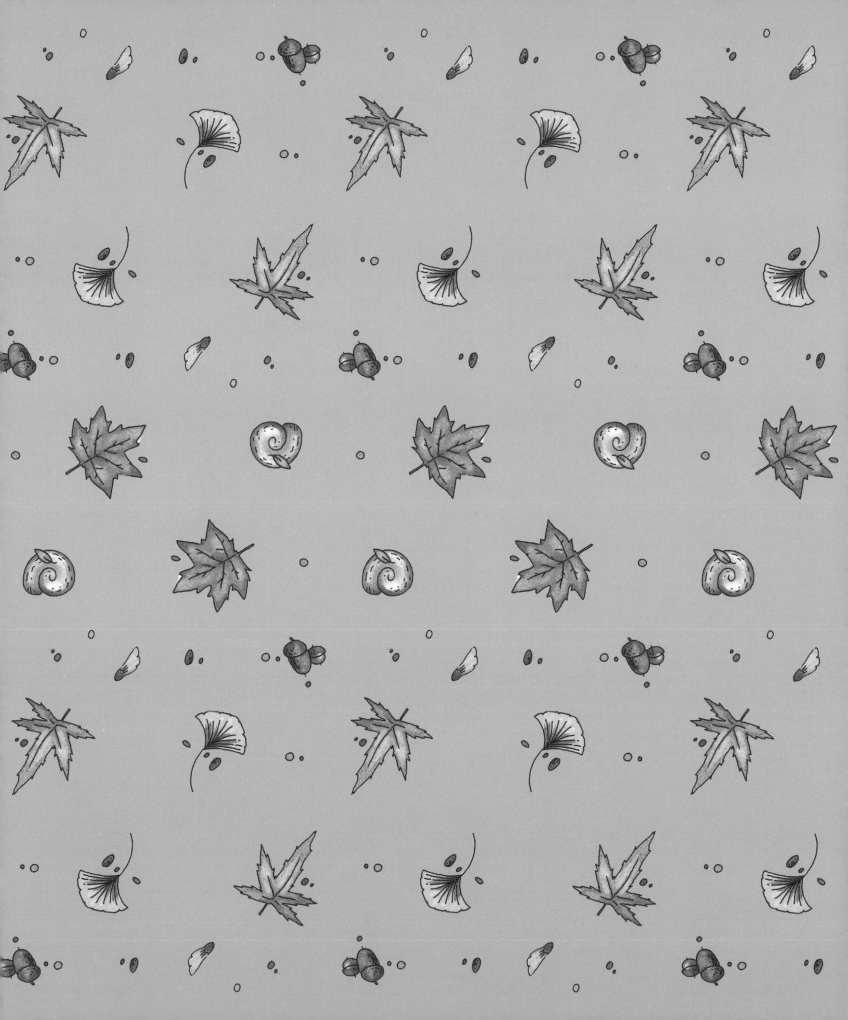

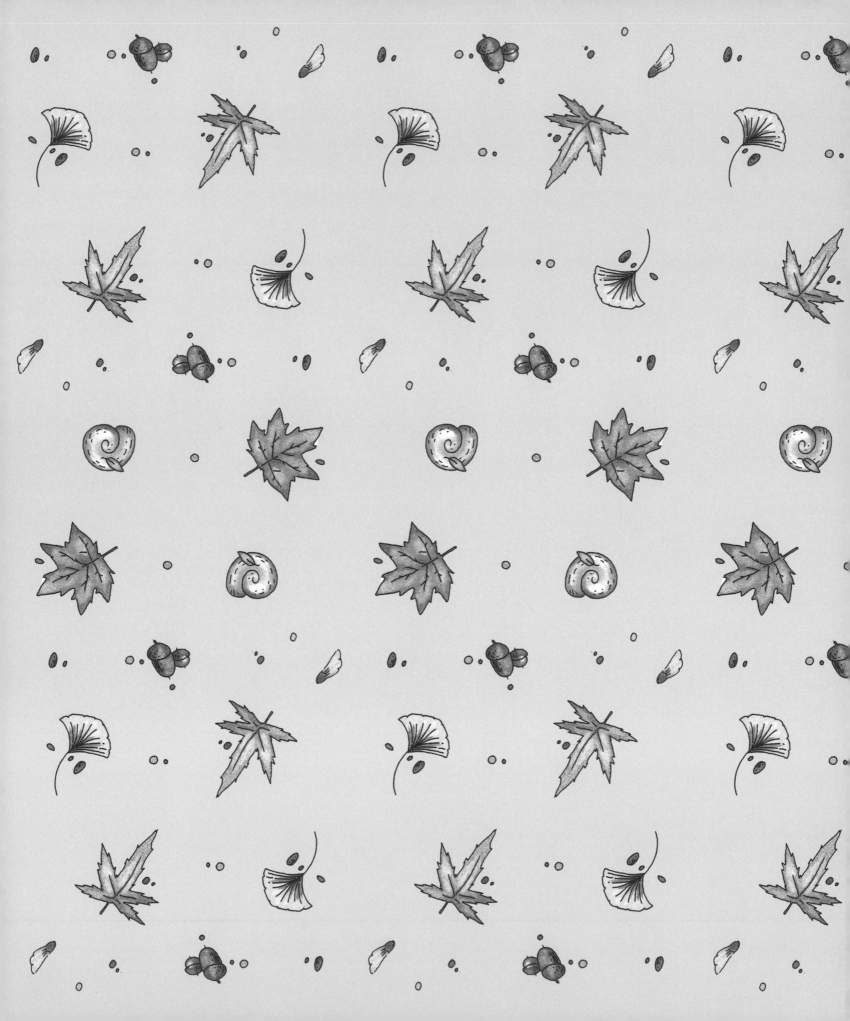